V
Loved One
is
Addicted

How to Offer Hope and Help

GREGORY L. JANTZ, PHD
WITH KEITH WALL

AspirePress

When a Loved One Is Addicted: How to Offer Hope and Help
© 2021 Gregory L. Jantz
Published by Aspire Press
An imprint of Hendrickson Publishing Group
Rose Publishing, LLC
P.O. Box 3473
Peabody, Massachusetts 01961-3473 USA
www.HendricksonPublishingGroup.com

ISBN 978-162862-988-0

Images used under license from Shutterstock.com: fizkes cover, p. 3, 5, 9, 34, 37, 57, 81, 101; laaisee p. 7; Tero Vesalainen p. 11; Elena Shashkina p. 22; alphaspirit.it p. 39; Olaf Holland p. 41; Prostock-studio p. 43, 79; Asier Romero p. 44; Olivier Le Moal p. 47; Ann Patchanan p. 48; Joel Everard p. 51; SvetaZi p. 52; lassedesignen p. 54; Pixelvario p. 60; Denis Belitsky p. 63; KieferPix p. 65; Bartle Halpin p. 67; Thapana Apisariyakul p. 69; Nic Vilceanu p. 70; Fotyma p. 75; rospoint p. 77; Antonio Guillem p. 83; fongbeerredhot p. 88; Svetlana Feofanova p. 99; Love You Stock p. 102.

Printed in the United States of America
010421VP

Contents

The Battle Against Addiction

Anyone who has suffered the heartbreak of watching someone they love succumb to an addiction will agree that it feels like being trapped in a disorienting carnival hall of mirrors. Once you step inside, even your own reflection becomes distorted. Your footing feels treacherous, the way forward is confusing, and the way out begins to feel impossible to find. Every turn only leads deeper into a maze of dead ends and trap doors.

That's how it *feels*—but I'm happy to tell you, it's not the truth. Though there isn't a single map to guide us, every person *can* find a unique pathway through the fear, guilt, shame, and despair back into the light and fresh air of freedom.

How can I be so sure? The simplest answer to that question is also the most powerful: because God is the Great Healer, for whom *anything* is possible. As a Christian who has faced deep personal challenges of my own through the years, I know firsthand how true that is. As a mental health professional, I've seen this marvelous fact demonstrated countless times in the lives of those I've counseled. No matter what your story is, and no matter how convinced you are that there is no way out, God's healing grace is undiminished. You can be free of the harmful effects of a loved one's addiction. By grounding yourself in a clear understanding of what addiction is, how and why it takes hold in someone's life, and how to protect *yourself* while maintaining your love for them, you'll be far better equipped to offer appropriate help.

That's what this book provides—an introduction to the awareness you need to move forward in both truth *and* grace. Addiction is an enormous topic, far too complex for a single small volume like this one. Rather, this is meant to be a primer that lays the foundation for additional study and growth.

Before we begin, however, I must issue a warning: If what you hope to learn in the pages ahead is how to go about "rescuing" your addicted child, parent, spouse, sibling, friend, or other loved one—then you are likely to stumble a while longer in the maze. To truly find the exit, you must acknowledge and accept that it is not within your power to "fix" another person. Their journey is their own. Only *they* can choose to walk their personal path to freedom.

Al-Anon—the excellent support group for people just like you—has distilled this principle into a valuable tool called *The Three Cs.*

- You didn't *cause* the addiction.

- You can't *control* it.

- You can't *cure* it.

With these things firmly in mind, you'll finally be in a position to succeed at what you can do: love the addict unconditionally and be a positive presence in their life, guided by healthy boundaries that protect everyone. If that sounds like a solid step out of the maze you've been stuck in, I invite you to read on to learn *how.*

CHAPTER 1

Understanding Addiction

Harold and Diane sat in my office on a rainy, gray December afternoon. The feeble light coming through the windows perfectly matched the quality of their emotional reserves, dimmed after years of living with an addicted child. Their daughter, Deborah, was in another part of the building going through intake and orientation on day one at a Seattle-area treatment center. Her personal drug of choice was the opioid OxyContin, though that wasn't the only substance she used.

Harold and Diane were both clearly exhausted. This was the third time they'd dropped Deborah off at a treatment center in under two years. But it was still easy to see in their comments and body language the position each had staked out in relation to their daughter's addiction. As he sat down, Harold's eyes were still wet from crying in heart-wrenching grief as he had watched the doors close behind his "little girl." He said hopeful things to me like, "I'm certain your approach here will make all the difference. I know this time it will take."

Diane's expression, by contrast, was as hard and cold as the sky outside. She didn't even make eye contact with me or her husband for at least the first ten minutes of our time together. She mumbled a comment wondering, "Why should this time be any different?"

Side by side, they presented a clear example of two common and opposite approaches among people who must deal with addiction in someone they love. One sees only innocence, while the other sees only blame. One clings to every shred of hope, while the other is braced for more pain. One believes in "magic bullets," while the other has lost all faith in change.

Naturally, this is overly simplistic, describing the extreme reaches of a pendulum that can swing back and forth in the same person—sometimes in a single day! Still, it's instructive to consider these opposites and recognize a critically important truth: Neither approach is very helpful in resolving the pain of caring for an addict or in offering effective help.

Why? Because both indicate that a person has not yet embraced step number one on the journey back to health and well-being: acknowledging and accepting powerlessness. The famous twelve steps used by Alcoholics Anonymous have also been adopted by Al-Anon, the sister support group for people whose lives are affected by addiction. The first of those states, *"We admit we are powerless over alcohol (or any other substance or behavior)—that our lives have become unmanageable."*

Harold still believed that he had the power to "get through" to Deborah with the force of his selfless love and endless sacrifice and support. Diane was convinced of the same thing, but was sure the answer lay in strict discipline and hard-edged boundaries. Each still felt they could exert a measure of control over Deborah and her ability to choose healing.

Here's the point for you: The paradoxical result of giving all that up is a refreshing sense of comfort and even peace. An informal "Step Study" created by the leader of a Houston Al-Anon chapter expresses it like this:

- We were comforted to learn that we were powerless. It wasn't our fault. We couldn't be held responsible for a situation that was totally beyond our control.

- We took a hard look at our lives and realized that all our attempts to bring order into chaos, all our plans and schemes to make the alcoholic or addict confront his or her addiction, had failed. Our lives were unmanageable.

- We learned that we were not alone. All the people around the table with us were powerless, too. Their lives were, or had been, as big a mess as ours.

- By admitting that we were powerless to change the situation, we began to realize that we must release our loved one from all our attempts to control him or her. If we were powerless, then all our threats, pleas and iron determination were futile. We needed to let go and let God be in control. That moment of letting go brought with it freedom.

- We began to understand that when we let go of the efforts to change someone else, once we were free from that burden, we could begin to accept the changes in ourselves that were necessary to set us free.[1]

Over time, Harold and Diane came to understand that helping Deborah meant first helping themselves to be free of unrealistic and disempowering expectations—of themselves and their daughter. They educated themselves about the realities of addiction—its causes and characteristics—as a way to decouple their own well-being from vulnerability to Deborah's choices and to reclaim the power to manage the only thing they could: themselves.

What Is Addiction?

As I've said already, a comprehensive answer to that question would fill several books much longer than this one. However, for our purposes, we don't need to get overly technical. The American Psychiatric Association distills the description to this:

> People with addiction (severe substance use disorder) have an intense focus on using a certain substance(s), such as alcohol or drugs, to the point that it takes over their life. They keep using alcohol or a drug even when they know it will cause problems.[2]

One of the most common questions I'm asked—usually coming from people at the end of their rope—is this: "Why can't they see the harm this causes? What it's doing to their life? To *our* lives?"

The truth is, an addict is not blind. He or she often sees the consequences of their choices very well. But the nature of addiction guarantees that their need for the feeling a substance or behavior delivers will always eclipse every other consideration. A fifty-five-year-old man under my care once explained this condition with brutal honesty. "You need to understand something," he said during a family therapy session. "When I need a fix, I'm not choosing between the promise I made you last week and the drug. That promise doesn't exist. You don't exist. Getting what I need isn't just all that matters—it's all there *is*."

Traits and Telltales

According to the American Society of Addiction Medicine (ASAM), addiction is characterized by:

- **Inability to consistently abstain.** Even when you know you should say *no*, you keep saying *yes*.

- **Impairment in behavioral control.** The addiction takes over what you do and say, causing you to become a different person than you were.

- **Diminished recognition of significant problems with one's behaviors and interpersonal relationships.** You lose the ability to see how the addiction is ruining your life and relationships.

- **Craving.** Having is never enough. Instead, you are left constantly wanting.

- **A dysfunctional emotional response.** Your emotions aren't in line with what is really happening and you're unable to figure out what your responses should be.

ASAM goes on to say, "Like other chronic diseases, addiction often involves cycles of relapse and remission. Without treatment or engagement in recovery activities, addiction is progressive and can result in disability or premature death."[3] Addiction doesn't go away on its own. It doesn't get better. It gets worse. Pretending addiction doesn't exist ensures it does.

But, as helpful as official definitions can be, they often don't fully capture the reality of what it's like to *live* with all those things. Here are four of the harsh conditions and attitudes you can expect from someone who is addicted.

1 Trust is next to impossible.

In fact, this is the predictable result of everything else on this list. Accordingly, it deserves a place at the head of the line because, under perfect circumstances, genuine trust between people is hard to come by. In the absence of genuine and sustained recovery, an addict's behavior will always leave room for doubt.

2 You'll always be no better than second place.

In truth, even that is misleading, because it implies you're at least in the race. As I've already said, the harsh reality is that, the demands of dependency nearly always displace everything else completely.

3 Addicts are crazy-makers.

Someone suffering a substance abuse disorder will say and do nearly anything—distorting the truth or inventing false realities—to cover their need and their actions. This often leaves others disoriented and unsure if maybe they themselves might be the ones with a problem.

4 An addict's "friends" are often unsavory.

To an addict, friendships arise around a common need for drugs and achieving the common goal of access to them. That means they gravitate toward other addicts and drug dealers—not a source of comfort for the people who care for them.

These and other things are part of the reason why loving an addict and working to help them be free is so hard.

Endless Addictive Agents in Our Modern Era

Over the three decades of my work as a mental health expert, I've seen a change in how people view what constitutes addiction. Substances such as alcohol and illicit drugs have commonly been associated with addiction, but right before I founded The Center, singer Karen Carpenter died in 1983 from anorexia. I remember the collective shock that behaviors involving food could be addictive. Her death caused people to consider that other things could harbor the potential for addiction beyond a pill or a bottle.

As research has expanded, along with a better understanding of brain chemistry and other physiological factors, mental health authorities have added more and more addictions in the *Diagnostic and Statistical Manual of Mental Disorders* (DSM), the recognized guidebook in the field. Activities known as behavioral or process addictions have been added alongside substance addictions. As one expert said, "Behavioral science experts believe that all entities capable of stimulating a person can be addictive; and whenever a habit changes into an obligation, it can be considered as an addiction."[4]

A dictionary might define addiction as a strong compulsion to have or do something harmful. To me, the "have" points to substances and the "do" points to behaviors. Listing all the things capable of causing addiction would take more space than this book has. However, I want to highlight some of the more common ones that ensnare people.

Addictive Substances

Alcohol

I believe that alcohol is neither inherently good nor bad. It is a neutral substance, with the trouble coming from how a person uses it—in a strictly limited medicinal capacity, to getting totally drunk, or somewhere in between. The difficulty for some comes also from how their body reacts to alcohol.

But let's not minimize the individual and societal problems created by alcohol misuse or abuse. The word *epidemic* is justified in describing the prevalence of alcoholism and problem drinking, with its staggering consequences in loss of life, fractured families, and healthcare costs.

How do you know if you or someone you love has crossed a line toward addiction? One simple way is for an individual to answer the simple and long-standing CAGE Questionnaire.

- Have you ever felt you needed to **C**ut down on your drinking?

- Have people **A**nnoyed you by criticizing your drinking?

- Have you ever felt **G**uilty about drinking?

- Have you ever felt you needed a drink first thing in the morning (**E**ye-opener) to steady your nerves or to get rid of a hangover? [5]

According to the National Institute on Alcohol Abuse and Alcoholism, answering yes to two of these questions is considered "clinically significant."[6] In my experience, answering yes to even one can indicate how close a person is to the line between harmless and harmful.

Narcotics

The term *narcotics* covers a broad spectrum of substances that affect mood or behavior. They include both naturally occurring opioids and opiates, such as opium, morphine, and heroin, as well as those synthetically produced, such as OxyContin and its generic, oxycodone, hydrocodone, Demerol, Percodan, or any number of branded or generic pharmaceuticals. These narcotics can be used to produce a euphoric effect, but they are often used to relieve pain. The balance between good and bad in relation to these substances is razor thin. As one medical professional testified before Congress:

> It is estimated that between 26.4 million and 36 million people abuse opioids worldwide, with an estimated 2.1 million people in the United States suffering from substance use disorders related to prescription opioid pain relievers in 2012 and an estimated 467,000 addicted to heroin. The consequences of this abuse have been devastating and are on the rise. For example, the number of unintentional overdose deaths from prescription pain relievers has soared in the United States, more than quadrupling since 1999.[7]

Prescription and Over-the-Counter Medication

After marijuana and alcohol, prescription and over-the-counter (OTC) drugs are the most commonly abused substances by Americans fourteen and older.[8] The National Institute on Drug Abuse includes opioids under commonly abused drugs, but also lists categories such as:

- Central nervous system depressants, like Valium or Xanax;

- Stimulants, like dextroamphetamines and amphetamines, along with methylphenidates like Ritalin or Concerta; and

- Sedatives (barbiturates) and tranquilizers.

Having a prescription written by a doctor does not protect people from abusing such medication, especially when they don't follow the physician's medication orders. A Stanford University study showed that "over 60 percent of Americans don't follow doctors' orders in taking prescription meds."[9]

Good drugs—and not just prescribed medications—can become harmful for a variety of reasons. I've also seen misuse occur in OTC medication. For example, I've met people, without colds, who buy cold medicine to use as a sedative or to get high through either the cough suppressant ingredient or simply the alcohol content. I've seen people who are addicted to diet pills or laxatives. Even motion sickness medication, such as Dramamine or Benadryl, can be used to produce a high.

Tobacco

Information about the harmful effects of smoking and nicotine has been known for half a century. Yet according to the Centers for Disease Control and Prevention (CDC), 15 percent of US adults smoke and "cigarette smoking is the leading cause of preventable disease and death in the United States, accounting for more than 480,000 deaths every year, or 1 of every 5 deaths."[10]

Despite the warnings, people continue to use tobacco because it is addictive. I've worked with people who are addicted to a variety of substances and have been told numerous times by them that it was more difficult to quit cigarettes than hard drugs such as heroin.

Food

Food is a powerful mood-altering substance. I say that as a person who works with healthcare professionals and dietitians schooled in the intricate connections between the food we eat and the way we feel. As a certified eating disorder specialist, I know that a relatively small number of people are diagnosed with eating disorders. The statistics from the National Association of Anorexia Nervosa and Associated Disorders (ANAD) puts the numbers at just under 1 percent of women over their lifetimes for anorexia, 1.5 percent of women over their lifetimes for bulimia, and 2.8 percent of all adults from binge eating disorder over their lifetimes.[11] However, I've found that too many people struggle

FOOD IS PERHAPS THE MOST READILY AVAILABLE AND SOCIALLY ACCEPTABLE MOOD-ALTERING SUBSTANCE THERE IS.

with their weight. They struggle with using food for all sorts of reasons that have nothing to do with nutrition. Food is perhaps the most readily available and socially acceptable mood-altering substance there is.

Addictive Behaviors

Behavioral addictions do not involve substances, but they can be just as powerful and difficult to manage. Here are a few of the most common.

Gambling

A gambling addiction is all about payoff, but the payoff can be more than just money. For many people, the dependency becomes the adrenaline rush and potentially euphoric feeling of hitting the jackpot. For others, gambling's payoff may be more about the thrill of risk. Winning or losing isn't the issue; playing the game of chance is. The euphoric "hit" that gambling produces comes from their own brain chemicals, primarily dopamine. Gambling feels good because your brain is wired to produce dopamine during pleasurable activities.

Sex

For people addicted to sex and sexual activities, the satisfaction is too fleeting and the feeling must be addressed again—immediately. Some have described their sexual addictions as insatiable. Engaging in sexual activities makes them crave even more. To engage in the sexual activity of their choice, they will reorder their priorities until every other part of their lives becomes subordinate to sexual gratification.

People I've counseled with sex addictions are often bewildered that their addiction has taken such control over their lives. They are humiliated by what they've done to satisfy sexual cravings, deeply shameful they are so enslaved to these activities.

Relationships

Relationship addiction is a condition where a person must either be in or pursuing a relationship to feel good about themselves or to avoid feeling bad about themselves. They derive their sense of identity and purpose through a relationship, which is a primary way of coping with life. People who develop relationship dependency crave validation and a sense of wholeness they believe can only come from another person.

Technology and Digital Devices

In recent years, we've heard a lot about digital addiction, sometimes called Internet addiction or Problematic Internet Use (PIU). Though a relatively new phenomenon, researchers and social scientists agree that dependency on digital devices is an actual addiction with similar symptoms and repercussions to other addictions, including substance abuse. Numerous studies published in respected, peer-reviewed scientific journals have demonstrated the link between digital addiction and many other mental health issues, including depression and anxiety. For example, a study reported by the Anxiety and Depression Association of America (ADAA) said:

> In a recent analysis of 2006 patients, 181 (9 percent) of which had moderate to severe problematic Internet use, it was found that attention-deficit hyperactivity disorder (ADHD) and social anxiety disorder were associated with high PIU scores in young participants (over age 25), whereas generalized anxiety disorder (GAD) and obsessive-compulsive disorder (OCD) were associated with high PIU scores in the older participants respectively.[12]

Technology can be helpful in providing information, efficiencies, and enjoyment. But overuse and addiction to technology can cause serious issues to a person's relationships, job, and health. The "rush" a person experiences from technology produces the same chemical reaction in the brain that stimulants like heroin produce. Dopamine is released when we have a pleasurable experience, and the body begins to crave that sensation. If we cause that release in excess over time through prolonged technology use, our body becomes conditioned and will reduce its natural production of dopamine because it is being substituted by the unnatural production stimulated by the external sources.

Pornography

A few years ago, pornography rates made the news when a Barna Group study reported that "64 percent of Christian men and 15 percent of Christian women admitted to viewing pornography at least once a month, compared to 65 percent of men and 30 percent of women who identified as non-Christian and said they watched porn at the same rate."[13]

At The Center, we treat people struggling with pornography who have all the hallmarks of classic addiction—compulsion to engage, withdrawal when not engaged, tolerance, mood modification, and inability to cut down or stop even when faced with negative consequences. Pornography, like sex addiction, can be shrouded in secrecy and tangled with an addiction to technology and the Internet.

In Search of the Elusive "Why?"

Why do some people succumb to addiction while others don't? That is among the most frustrating questions we face when dealing with the effects of addiction on someone we love. That's because it has too many answers—none of them definitive. To be fair, researchers continue to do their best to find a "Holy Grail" explanation, because that might also suggest a consistent, reliable treatment.

In the meantime, let's briefly examine five factors known to play a role in the development of addiction.

(1) Past Trauma

Many studies have established a significant link between exposure to traumatic stress during childhood or adolescence and the development of substance abuse disorders. Here is a summary from the National Child Traumatic Stress Network:

- Although it is unclear exactly how many adolescents who abuse drugs or alcohol also have experienced trauma, numerous studies have documented a correlation between trauma exposure and substance abuse in adolescents.

- Teens who had experienced physical or sexual abuse/assault were three times more likely to report past or current substance abuse than those without a history of trauma.

- In surveys of adolescents receiving treatment for substance abuse, more than 70 percent of patients had a history of trauma exposure. This correlation is particularly strong for adolescents with PTSD. Studies indicate that up to 59 percent of young people with PTSD subsequently develop substance abuse problems.[14]

It's not hard to see why someone who has suffered a traumatic event—physical or sexual abuse, severe neglect, exposure to violence, and so on—would turn to self-medication with substances as a coping strategy. What is less clear is why for some this leads to long-term struggle with addiction, while others eventually choose more healthy outlets.

2 Multiple Conditions

We've built our entire treatment philosophy around what I call the "whole-person approach." That is, we recognize that when someone seeks help for one type of mental disorder, chances are good that others also exist alongside it. For instance, depression and anorexia go hand in hand, as do PTSD and anxiety. A number of lifestyle imbalances can contribute, such as diet, quantity and quality of sleep, time spent engaged with electronic devices, social isolation, and lack of exercise.

This is just as true in cases of addiction. People struggling with a substance abuse disorder frequently suffer from a mood disorder as well, such as depression, anxiety, and bipolar disorder. An article in *Psychology Today* describes the connection:

> It was once believed by many that alcohol and drug addiction recovery should be addressed apart from mental illnesses. While others did see that co-occurring substance use and mood disorders have negative crossover effects that complicate addiction recovery, the relationship between these disorders was not well understood. More and more, this concept is changing, and people affected by addictive substance use are more thoroughly assessed for mood disorders while in treatment.[15]

3 Physiology and Brain Chemistry

Addictions of all kinds affect the brain's production of neurotransmitters, such as dopamine. It is released in what has been called the brain's pleasure center—

the nucleus accumbens. Medical experts describe the process this way:

> Generally speaking, when you experience a positive sensation and dopamine is released into the pathways of the reward center, your brain takes note of: What triggered the sensation. Was it a substance? A behavior? A type of food? Any cues from your environment that can help you find it again. Did you experience it at night? What else were you doing? Were you with a certain person? When you're exposed to those environmental cues, you'll begin to feel the same drive to seek out that same pleasure. This drive can be incredibly powerful, creating an urge that's hard to control.[16]

 4 **Genetics**

A growing body of research is making it clear that genetics play an important role in a person's risk of addiction. According to the National Institute on Drug Abuse, "Family studies that include identical twins, fraternal twins, adoptees, and siblings suggest that as much as half of a person's risk for becoming addicted to nicotine, alcohol, or other drugs depends on his or her genetic makeup."[17]

The key word here is *risk*, not *surety*. Some people's genetic makeup places them at a higher risk for cancer or Parkinson's disease or sickle cell anemia. Whether they actually contract the disease depends on many other factors as well. But by being aware of the increased risk, they can adopt lifestyle and behavioral changes to improve their odds of staying healthy. The same can be said of anyone who knows that addiction is part of their own genetic heritage.

5 Personality Traits

Many scientists are reluctant to put stock in the existence of an "addictive personality." That's because no one has yet discovered conclusive evidence. Experts generally consider addiction to be a disorder of the brain, not a personality issue.

Nevertheless, the idea persists. Some of the personality traits loosely associated with substance abuse are impulsivity, lack of restraint, lower regard for social conventions, poor risk assessment, manipulative tendencies, and sensation-seeking. None of these are set in stone, of course. Yet it's helpful to know what the personality "default" setting is for your loved one. Once you understand their tendencies, given their personality, you can help them learn skills to choose a different direction.

You Are Not Alone

The point of starting this conversation about how to cope with addiction in someone you love is simple: *encouragement and empowerment!*

Chances are you've seen some or all of these characteristics and behaviors in your loved one. Maybe you've struggled to understand it all without this valuable context: *You are not alone.* I hope this discussion has demonstrated that science, and the experience of others who have walked the path before you, are on your side.

> "I WILL EXALT YOU, LORD, FOR YOU LIFTED ME OUT OF THE DEPTHS. ... I CALLED TO YOU FOR HELP, AND YOU HEALED ME. YOU, LORD, BROUGHT ME UP FROM THE REALM OF THE DEAD; YOU SPARED ME FROM GOING DOWN TO THE PIT."
>
> Psalm 30:1-3

Now let's turn from understanding addiction in general to considering information that's much more personal—how addiction works in the person you love and how it affects the entire family.

THE SCOPE OF ADDICTIONS

It's a well-known fact that addictions of all kinds afflict or affect millions of people across the country. But many don't realize the tragic scope of the problem. Here is a snapshot of statistics compiled by the Addiction Center:

- Almost 21 million Americans have at least one addiction, yet only 10 percent of them receive treatment.

- Drug overdose deaths have more than tripled since 1990.

- From 1999 to 2017, more than 700,000 Americans died from a drug overdose.

- Alcohol and drug addiction cost the US economy over $600 billion every year.

- In 2017, 34.2 million Americans committed DUI, 21.4 million under the influence of alcohol and 12.8 million under the influence of drugs.

- Approximately 20 percent of Americans who have depression or an anxiety disorder also have a substance use disorder.

- More than 90 percent of people who have an addiction started to drink alcohol or use drugs before they were 18 years old.

- Americans between the ages of 18 and 25 are most likely to use addictive drugs.

- About 6 percent of American adults (about 15 million people) have an alcohol use disorder, but only about 7 percent of Americans who are addicted to alcohol ever receive treatment.

- About 130 Americans die every day from an opioid overdose.

- About 30 percent of people who regularly use marijuana have a marijuana use disorder.

- About 5 million Americans are regular cocaine users.[18]

WHAT TO WATCH FOR

The American Society of Addiction Medicine (ASAM) defines addiction as a chronic disease that affects the brain's reward, motivation, and memory functions. Someone with an addiction will crave a substance or other behavioral habits. The person will often ignore other areas of life to fulfill or support the compulsion.[19]

Your loved one might be struggling with addiction if he or she:

☐ Fails to fulfill obligations at work, home, or school.

☐ Sleeps too much or too little, compared with previous sleep patterns.

☐ Exhibits changes in personality and mood, such as a lack of motivation, irritability, depression, and agitation.

☐ Is often secretive and deceitful: lying, stealing, and sneaking around.

☐ Continues with a behavior despite ongoing problems caused or worsened by its use.

☐ Has developed tolerance, which means needing more and more of the addictive agent or activity to achieve the desired effects.

☐ Is financially unpredictable or irresponsible: not paying bills, borrowing money, or incurring large debt.

☐ Minimizes the effects of the behavior ("It's no big deal") or claims the ability to stop the behavior ("I can stop any time I want to. I just don't want to!").

☐ Shows signs of withdrawal, which happens when the person stops taking the substance or engaging in the activity. The signs can include sweating, shaking, agitation, constant fidgeting, nausea, or vomiting.

☐ Has lost interest in activities once enjoyed and pursued.

☐ Exhibits changes in energy—unexpectedly and extremely tired or energetic.

☐ Has experienced dramatic weight loss or weight gain.

☐ Frequently has bloodshot and glazed eyes and/or bloody noses.

☐ Changed friends and social groups, now associating with people you consider questionable or concerning.

☐ Repeatedly has unexplained outings and offering excuses for activities that don't add up.

CHAPTER 2

Understanding the Addict in Your Life

Addiction may seek to isolate the addict, but its consequences are anything but isolated. They leach out and contaminate surrounding relationships. Addiction promotes and perpetuates false beliefs, which can affect not only the addicted person but also others. Because of this, addiction has the capacity to transmit itself from person to person through the pathway of experienced pain.

Living in the midst of addiction leaves family members feeling traumatized and overwhelmed. They've been lied to, betrayed, and manipulated. There are arguments and confrontations, slamming doors, and sleepless nights. Often, there's more serious trouble such as an accident, a lost job, or an arrest. Or even worse still, fear of overdose or death.

The title of a *Psychology Today* article highlights this issue: "Addiction Is a Family Affliction." The author writes,

> The addiction of a loved one brings up many difficult questions that may leave you unable to understand what is happening and why, and feeling like you are riding an emotional rollercoaster and you can't get off. You may find yourself struggling with a number of painful and conflicting emotions, including guilt, shame, self-blame, frustration, anger, sadness, depression, anxiety, and fear. ... No one comes into this world knowing how to deal effectively with the addiction of a loved one.[20]

It's important to understand the motivations, thought processes, and emotional drives of the addicted individual. When you gain insight into the addict's struggle, you will be better equipped to offer help and hope in a way that honors yourself in the process.

Fears That Fuel Addiction

Many family members initially wonder why their addicted loved one can't just stop. They might believe the problem could be overcome if the person tried harder, had more self-control, prayed more fervently, or trusted God more.

It's true that tenacity, fortitude, and faith are essential, but addiction is a deeply rooted problem with strong emotional undercurrents that keep many people stuck in their chronic compulsion. Let's look at four fears that fuel addiction.

1 Fear of Failure

To admit an addiction is to admit powerlessness, as reflected in step one of Alcoholics Anonymous' twelve-step recovery program. In our culture, we are taught to be self-sufficient, to assert our independence and autonomy in all kinds of situations. Whatever the circumstances, we strive to become masters of our fates and captains of our souls.

So imagine the sense of failure when an addiction becomes both captain and master, making a person a servant and slave to his cravings. Acknowledging that addiction has made life unmanageable is to also acknowledge that willpower, attempts at self-control, and having more faith in God won't cure the disease of dependency. Almost universally, a true acknowledgment

LIVING IN THE MIDST OF ADDICTION LEAVES FAMILY MEMBERS FEELING TRAUMATIZED AND OVERWHELMED.

of addiction is quickly followed by a crushing sense of personal failure, whether initially expressed or not.

A sense of failure creates a suffocating cloud of shame. For some people caught in addiction, shame is the demon they've been running from their entire lives. Since as long as they can remember, they've felt defective and inadequate, and have run from being labeled as such. The addiction has served as an escape from shame's relentless pursuit, a substance- or behavior-induced time-out.

2 Fear of Exposure

None of us likes to be totally exposed—to be caught doing something embarrassing, to have our shortcomings revealed, to feel like we're on stage for the world to see. Each of us projects an image that enables us to be viewed as *okay* or *acceptable* by other people. For addicts, who know their inner world is not okay and their lifestyle is not acceptable, fear of exposure further compels them to anesthetize their painful emotions by pursuing more of their addictive agent.

In some ways, we live in a "fine" world. "How are you?" "I'm fine, thank you, and you?" "I'm fine too." We all want to be fine because we think we should be, but we're not. We're in pain, we're distressed, we're overwhelmed, we're addicted, but we don't want anyone to know because admitting any of those things means we've failed the "fine test." If we admit to being not fine, we expose our faults, problems, and weaknesses.

AT THE ROOT OF THE FEAR OF REJECTION IS THE QUESTION, "WILL YOU STILL LOVE ME?"

3   Fear of Rejection

Admitting an addiction can be extraordinarily difficult because of the terrifying possibility of rejection by others. It can seem like walking over hot coals—a prolonged

journey of excruciating pain as the person anticipates incredulous, agonized, or disgusted reactions.

At the root of the fear of rejection is the question, "Will you still love me?" In some cases, the answer has been *no*. Because people have the free will to reject that relationship, *no* is an ever-present possibility. However, *no* happens much less frequently than addiction's apocalyptic prophecies to the contrary.

Loved ones have already borne the brunt of much of the addiction's effects, whether those loved ones are aware of the actual addiction. The estrangement, jealousy, chaos, and altered reality have all damaged the

> FOR I AM THE LORD YOUR GOD WHO TAKES HOLD OF YOUR RIGHT HAND AND SAYS TO YOU, DO NOT FEAR; I WILL HELP YOU."
>
> Isaiah 41:13

relationship. The underlying reasons may not be clear, but the relationships have already experienced significant erosion. The addiction will argue that telling the truth is sure to cause the remaining relationship foundation to cave in and crumble.

 ## 4 Fear of Change

As the saying goes, "Better the devil you know than the devil you don't." In other words, it's better to deal with something known, even though it's not good, than risk dealing with something different that could be worse. This is the essence of pessimistic thinking because it assumes that something different is going to be something worse. Addiction is a prolific pessimist.

Addressing the problem of addiction will inevitably lead to changes—significant, life-altering changes. The addict may think:

- I'll lose my friends.

- I'll lose my job.

- I'll ruin my reputation.

- I won't have any fun.

- I won't know what to do with myself.

- This is just the way I am.

Most of all, the addict thinks:

- What would my life be like without drugs [or alcohol or gambling or pornography]? That's a change I'm not willing to make.

The assumption is that a different life will be worse because non-addictive strategies to cope with that different life will be less effective. Therefore, the future should be feared because change is bad. Addictive thinking may admit that the devil you know is bad, but the devil you don't—change—is worse.

Barriers to Healing

A dictionary definition of addiction is simple: a strong compulsion to have or do something harmful. Simple— or is it? Who defines what is harmful? And to whom? Addiction constructs barriers to answering questions about what is harmful.

 1 ## The Barrier of Denial

Denial is a state in which a person disavows or distorts what is really happening. He might ignore the problem, shrug off people's concerns, or blame others for any issue.

DENIAL IS A STATE IN WHICH A PERSON DISAVOWS OR DISTORTS WHAT IS REALLY HAPPENING.

In terms of addiction, denial is a powerful coping mechanism to delay facing the truth and therefore delay taking helpful action.

This is why confronting an addict is like rolling the dice. Some addicts flatly refuse to consider even the remote possibility of a problem. Others dissolve into a mass of recriminations, tears, and despair. Still others agree to entertain the notion while attempting to negotiate continuing the destructive behavior.

There is a reason speakers at an Alcoholics Anonymous (AA) meeting begin with "Hello, my name is … and I'm an alcoholic." Admitting such a truth publicly catapults the person over the barrier of denial. Once the person has accepted that addiction is part of his life, he can use that truth to dictate what part the addiction will play in his life going forward.

2　The Barrier of Secrecy

Did you ever break something when you were a kid? A drinking glass or a lamp? If you were like me, the first thing you did was look around to see if anyone noticed. Next, you tried to hide the damage so it wouldn't be discovered. Addicts are highly skilled at finding ways to hide because addiction thrives in secrecy.

Secrecy provides cover, both to the addict and to the addiction, but secrecy's benefits are not the same for each. Secrecy allows the addiction to reveal what it truly is. Secrecy does not act to restrain the addiction; instead, it provides a platform of noninterference, a free-for-all. While secrecy allows the addiction to reveal what it is, secrecy allows the addict to hide who he is. An addiction feels no shame or remorse, but an addict can and will. Addicts think being exposed is harmful, so they act in secret.

A phrase used often in AA says, "You're only as sick as your secrets." That means that a secret kept in the dark grows and becomes more entrenched and damaging. But once it is brought into the light or released, it loses its power.

3 The Barrier of Minimizing

When the thing you broke as a kid was eventually discovered, you could no longer keep the destruction secret. Your only option was to minimize the damage: "We have plenty of glasses." "No one will notice the scratch if I turn the lamp this way." You used any excuse to try to avoid the consequences, which experience taught you were going to be negative.

The consequences of trying to minimize an addiction, however, are far more severe than a broken glass or a scratched lamp. Unfortunately, as a person gets older, addiction can cause more destruction, but addicts can become more adept at minimizing the destruction. If the addiction is brought up, the person may act like you're blowing things out of proportion or exaggerating. She might say things like, "It's not that bad," "Other people do way more than I do," or "So what? It's not like I'm hurting anybody!"

While minimizing seeks to make the addiction seem less than it is, maximizing makes the addiction seem more than it is—more powerful, inevitable, and insurmountable. Maximizing is also called catastrophic thinking. "Catastrophic thinking can be defined as ruminating about irrational worst-case outcomes. Needless to say, it can increase anxiety and prevent people from taking action in a situation where action is required."[21]

> **MINIMIZING SEEKS TO MAKE THE ADDICTION SEEM LESS THAN IT IS, MAXIMIZING MAKES THE ADDICTION SEEM MORE THAN IT IS.**

In the defeatist thinking of maximizing, the addiction is so big that it's already won and attempting to change is a lost cause. The future becomes defined in failure, with success no longer attainable. "This is just the way I am" becomes the rationale for staying trapped within the addiction, which becomes the new normal. In their view, they'll never overcome the addiction, so they'll learn to live with it.

The renowned psychologist Carl Jung once said, "Shame is a soul-eating emotion." I agree. I've found that shame is one of the driving forces behind addiction and one of the primary barriers that prevents recovery. There can be deep shame in admitting you are not in control and the addiction is.

THERE CAN BE DEEP SHAME IN ADMITTING YOU ARE NOT IN CONTROL AND THE ADDICTION IS.

One of the world's leading researchers on shame, Dr. Brené Brown, says, "I define shame as the intensely painful feeling or experience of believing that we are flawed and therefore unworthy of love and belonging. I don't believe shame is helpful or productive. In fact, shame is much more likely to be the source of destructive, hurtful behavior than the solution or cure. I think the fear of disconnection can make us dangerous."[22]

It's no wonder, then, that shame is an isolating, debilitating emotion that causes deep-seated self-doubt and unworthiness. While almost everyone experiences these feelings at one point or another, some individuals aren't able to escape it, with these emotions being a daily destructive companion. For those in active addiction, shame isn't just an occasional occurrence; it's something experienced almost continually.

In active addiction, feelings of shame can seem almost unbearable. The chronic sense of unworthiness and inferiority make an addicted person believe he isn't worthy of love, respect, or even happiness. The person becomes ashamed of who they are and, as a result, depression, hopelessness, and numbness become chronic.

Family Members Become Collateral Damage

Addiction is often thought of as a disease that affects a single person—the one who is dependent on and unable to break free from a substance or behavior. This is an understandable misconception. The life of the addicted person becomes clearly unmanageable as the dependency progresses. We see the person's life fall apart, manifested by loss of jobs, relationships, physical health, mental stability, and social connections.

But how are the lives of the family members affected by the addiction of their loved ones? For many families, this question is ignored and overlooked for a long time, as the focus of attention is on the addict himself. The truth is, however, that addiction of a loved one has a drastic effect on the family as a whole. In fact, the National Council On Alcoholism And Drug Dependence describes addiction as "a family disease that stresses the family to the breaking point, impacts the stability of the home, the family's unity, mental health, physical health, finances, and overall family dynamics."[23]

Simply put, family members become collateral damage, suffering different though dramatic consequences along with the addict. Those people connected to the addict— and by extension, to the addiction—get caught in the undercurrent of damage.

Here are just a few ways family members often feel.

Lonely

For spouses, parents, or children, one of the most common forms of collateral damage is loneliness. As the addiction consumes greater amounts of their loved one's time, energy, and attention, they find themselves crowded out, abandoned to live a life alone or subservient to the addiction. Their own needs, wants, and desires are boxed out, placed on hold.

Family members often experience the physical absence of the addict because the person is off somewhere acquiring or using the drug of choice. More often, family members feel the emotional and intellectual absence even when the addict is physically present. That is because the person's thoughts are someplace else, his emotions are numbed, and his energy is low. All of this leaves everyone around the addict to feel distant and alone, even when together.

PEOPLE CONNECTED TO THE ADDICT ... GET CAUGHT IN THE UNDERCURRENT OF DAMAGE.

Deceived

Anyone who has been around an active addict knows that he or she is a master liar. Active addicts have perfected the "con" to a fine art, and the lies typically happen on three levels:

- **Addicts lie to themselves.** The purpose of this lying is to stay out of touch with what they are feeling and what they know and need.

- **Addicts lie to people around them.** By doing so, they create a confusing and dishonest family system.

- **Addicts lie to the world at large.** They pretend to be something they're not, often putting up a good front to convince others that all is well.

This systematic deceptiveness leaves family members continually suspicious, mistrustful, and feeling duped. As a mother of a twenty-two-year-old alcoholic told me, "From one day to the next, from one moment to the next, I'm never sure if Derek is telling me the truth or telling me a blatant lie. There have been countless times when he's looked me straight in the eye and told me something, swearing up and down that it was the truth. I felt so stupid when I believed him and then his 'truth' turned out to be yet another lie. I want to believe the best about him, but how can I? He consistently tries to deceive his own mother."

ADDICTION IS A JEALOUS PRESENCE, TOLERATING NO CHALLENGE TO ITS SUPREMACY IN A PERSON'S LIFE.

Sadly, for any family member of an addict, this mother's feelings and experiences will sound very familiar.

Worth Less

The people closest to an addict feel "worth less" than the addictive agent (alcohol, drugs, gambling, and so on), which causes them to feel *worthless*. Addicts place priority on their behavior, at the expense of family members and others. Addiction is a jealous presence, tolerating no challenge to its supremacy in a person's life.

This sense of worthlessness is often felt most strongly when a child's relationship with a parent is undermined by that parent's addiction. The child does not understand the subtle pressures and complex motivations of the addiction. All he knows is that the parent fails to provide attention or affection. The voice of the addiction may even speak out against the child, transferring blame and guilt onto them. Children can assume the reason they are not being loved or cared for is because there is something inherently wrong with them.

Constant Chaos

The addict anxiously plots out the next encounter with the addiction, fearful and unsure of either the certainty of each occurrence or its ultimate effectiveness. The addict lives a life of uncertainty, which becomes subtly and overtly communicated to others.

Those associated with the addict also live lives of uncertainty, unsure what the next crisis will be and what it will require. Responding to crises can become so ingrained in their experiences, especially as children, that life without them can become a foreign experience and seem stressful. When crisis is the expected and anticipated norm of childhood, life is robbed of peace. Those in relationship with someone struggling with addiction end up struggling themselves, as their lives become entangled with the consequences of that addiction.

Helpless

Those associated with an addict recognize, by the addiction's supremacy, they have been rejected. This is the reality they've lived with every day of the addiction. They may have cried out in frustration, "If you loved me, you'd stop!" only to watch the addiction continue. They come to understand the intensity of their love is not sufficient to change the addiction. They can support the change, but they cannot mandate the change. This leaves them with an overwhelming sense of helplessness. And because this helplessness is painful to experience, they may harbor unresolved anger toward the addicted loved one.

Blinded By Addiction

Family members live daily with the harsh reality of the addiction, wondering, "Why can't my loved one see the damage being caused?" The addict, however, while actively listening to the voice of the addiction, can fail to recognize the damage being done to others. This isn't surprising because the addict often fails to recognize the damage being done *to himself.*

My first answer to the question "Why can't my loved one see?" is that the addict's mind is blinded. Whenever he tries to see beyond the veil of addiction, he is presented with all sorts of reasons why he's not really seeing what he's seeing and why others aren't really experiencing what they're feeling. Within the haze of addiction, the person can't see truth clearly.

My second answer is because the person doesn't want to see the truth. It's too painful, and avoiding pain is an overriding reason for addiction. He is afraid of seeing the truth about what his addiction has done to *you.*

Thankfully, amid all these difficult realities, there is good news: Change is possible, healing can happen, and relationships can be restored. In the pages ahead, we'll discuss how you can be an active participant in that recovery and restoration.

A SHARED EXPERIENCE

Trying to know how to best help an addicted loved one can feel like a lonely, isolating pursuit—like you're in the struggle all by yourself. The fact is, millions of Americans are currently or have been in the same situation, concerned about the addiction of someone close to them.

> "CONFESS YOUR SINS TO EACH OTHER AND PRAY FOR EACH OTHER SO THAT YOU MAY BE HEALED. THE PRAYER OF A RIGHTEOUS PERSON IS POWERFUL AND EFFECTIVE."
>
> James 5:16

Specifically, near half (46 percent) of US adults have a family member or close friend who has been addicted to drugs. And that figure does not account for other types of addictions that don't involve substances. So the "addicted loved one" saga is likely experienced in some form by a majority of Americans.

These findings come from a Pew Research Center study that found this issue cuts across gender, race, age, education levels, and even partisan lines—meaning that almost no one is immune to having a family member or close friend who struggles with addiction.[24]

How You Can Help Your Loved One

You can do this.

And you might help to save your loved one's life.

These are the two essential messages I want you to hear as we discuss the uncomfortable and often painful process of taking action to help the addicted family member in your life.

After all, you have likely been asking an extremely important question for months, years, or even decades: How can I help my loved one?

The details of my response to you will depend, to some extent, on the state of mind of the person with the addiction. Hopefully, your loved one is willing to admit there is an addiction problem and recognizes that change is needed. It's also possible that he or she is not yet willing to acknowledge the problem. Denial has taken root, and the person does not see the need for professional help.

Regardless of his or her current belief, the road ahead will not be easy. Recovering from addiction is not a straightforward matter of simply stopping the damaging behavior. In fact, even under the best of circumstances, recovery is often a matter of three steps forward and two steps back.

One of the most painful aspects of loving someone with an addiction is the feeling that you are powerless to help. The flip side of this coin—and equally painful—is the feeling that it is somehow within your power to "fix" your loved one, coupled with the experience of failing at that task over and over again. The truth that we touched on earlier bears repeating now that you are preparing to take action. Remind yourself often …

- ▨ "I didn't *cause* this addiction."

- ▨ "I can't *cure* it."

- ▨ "I can't *control* it."

Understanding and accepting these three powerful truths will help you as you consider your role in the recovery and healing of the addict you care about. And yet, while you cannot *make* your loved one change—or engage in recovery for them—there are things you can do to encourage and instigate change. Indeed, your love and support in their life can be a significant factor. Even with the delicacy involved in addiction and recovery, your involvement may be the difference between life and death for someone you love.

Self-Care

Truly, some of the best advice I can offer you is to first take care of yourself. This may come as a surprise and may even sound selfish, but think of it this way: What do airline attendants say when they recite the emergency protocols prior to takeoff? *First, put on your own mask, then help the child or elderly person next to you with their own.* That's because it's far more difficult to help a less-capable person when you're incapacitated yourself.

As the addict continually makes and breaks promises to herself and others, you may experience feelings of anger, frustration, guilt, betrayal and—as the lengthy battle continues—sheer exhaustion. Meanwhile, you may become so preoccupied with the desperate battle that you're unaware that your own health and well-being are deteriorating.

So I want you to be aware of the common signs of caregiver burnout. The Mayo Clinic suggests these nine signs to watch for:

1. Feeling overwhelmed or constantly worried

2. Often feeling tired

3. Too little or too much sleep

4. Gaining or losing weight

5. Becoming easily irritated or angry

6. Losing interest in activities you once enjoyed

7. Sadness

8. Frequent headaches or other physical ailments

9. Depression and/or anxiety[25]

To this list I would add feelings of embarrassment over your situation and feelings of hopelessness. You may find yourself troubled over what your friends and acquaintances must be thinking and suffering the darkness of despair, as though this affliction will never end. Now is the time to stand strong against burnout by planting this standard in the forefront of your mind: *It is neither selfish nor negligent of me to first take care of myself.*

You must maintain sound physical, mental, and emotional health to better enjoy life despite this ongoing battle—and to better help your loved one face up to and eventually conquer addiction. In *Beyond Addiction: How Science and Kindness Help People Change*, the authors explain the importance of self-care:

> How can you accept your loved one until she stops what she is doing? One way is to have your wellbeing not wholly depend on her, and by devoting energy to something outside of your concerns for her. When you take care of yourself, you build strength to both tolerate what you can't change and change what you can. At the same time, as a calmer, happier person, you will be contributing to an atmosphere that is conductive to the change you hope to see in your loved one, and you will be modeling healthy behaviors you wish for in your loved one.[26]

To help you overcome the inevitable stresses and prevent harmful burnout, begin today to make the following three practices a non-negotiable part of your life.

1   Make your health and well-being a priority.

Eat nourishing meals and stay hydrated with plenty of water throughout the day. Take a good multivitamin and mineral supplement, while limiting coffee, sugar, and processed foods.

> "I CAN DO ALL THIS THROUGH HIM WHO GIVES ME STRENGTH."
>
> Philippians 4:13

Get outdoor exercise: walk, run, bike, or hike at least 20–30 minutes, breathing deeply and enjoying the sun's natural vitamin D. Add some weight-bearing exercises such as push-ups, crunches, squats, and bicep curls to keep your muscles toned.

Some days, your situation may make you feel so weary and discouraged that self-care is the last thing you want to think about. But here's the secret: Such down times are when focused self-care is most needed and will do you the most good. So memorize and declare Philippians 4:13: "I can do all this through him who gives me strength."

2. Maintain activities that replenish you.

If you're not careful, dealing with an addicted loved one can preoccupy you to the extent that you forget about the activities that used to bring you relaxation and joy.

Helping your loved one does not mean giving up your own life. A big part of healthy self-care is keeping your own life going, continuing those activities that invigorate you and make you smile.

IT IS NEITHER SELFISH NOR NEGLIGENT OF ME TO FIRST TAKE CARE OF MYSELF.

Take a moment to identify in writing at least five activities that bring you joy. Going to a movie? Lunch with friends? It could be a massage or manicure, a hike in the hills, a day at the museum or the zoo, a picnic at the park, or volunteering at your

church or a local non-profit. Then begin scheduling these activities and following through. Maintaining your enjoyments is not selfish; it is vital to your well-being.

3. Enlist the support of others.

Living with addiction can make you feel isolated and alone. But all around you is a healthy array of people who are going through what you're facing. Studies have shown that social support can help you build resilience against stress and provide you with practical ideas for dealing with your loved one.

Do not hesitate to reach out to a counselor, pastor, or mentor for ongoing help and advice. This person can also refer you to relevant support groups that allow caregivers to voice their concerns and encourage one another. Both individual counseling and group support can give you healthy outlets to process your emotions and strengthen you for the challenges ahead.

Strategies to Avoid Enabling

Family and friends of addicts often do things that might appear, on the surface, to be compassionate. But in reality, those actions are actually fueling their loved one's addiction. These actions include things such as:

- Lying to your spouse's boss about why he or she called in sick.

- Picking up the slack at home so you don't have to confront your loved one about neglecting responsibilities.

- Not taking care of yourself because you are so busy caring for someone who won't take care of herself.

- Embracing a role as self-designated worrier or protector.

It's true that well-meaning family members frequently perpetuate their struggling loved one's problem through *enabling* actions. In short, enabling means doing things for a person that he would and could do for himself if he weren't mired in addiction. Anything you do that protects the addict from the consequences of his actions could be allowing him to deny the problem or delay a decision to get help.

Therefore, it's in his best interest to keep responsibilities on his shoulders and avoid shielding him from consequences. This involves the decision to show tough love by not aiding or abetting them in their addiction. This is not an easy task, as it defies your natural impulses. Your instinct is to help, but sometimes your attempts at *helping* end up *hurting* the troubled individual.

Enabling removes the natural consequences that will likely result from an addict's choices. Professionals warn against enabling because evidence shows that addicts who experience the painful consequences of their addiction have the most powerful incentive to change their lifestyle. It often takes "hitting rock bottom" for addicts to recognize that change is indeed necessary.

While enablers see their good intentions as the easy way out initially, desperation eventually sets in and the demands of addiction become burdensome over time. The family and friendship dynamics typically become skewed, with the sober loved ones increasingly taking on more responsibility and the addict increasingly bearing less responsibility. This builds resentment on both sides, as addicts expect that the overly responsible members will continue to compensate for the addict's ongoing irresponsibility.

To correct this imbalance, enablers must learn new coping mechanisms and ways of communicating with their struggling loved one. Consider these five strategies:

1. Stop doing anything that supports the person's current lifestyle.

Are you allowing your family member to skip out on household chores and responsibilities? Are you working and paying bills that he would be paying if he hadn't lost his job or missed work time? Are you providing free food and shelter, even when the person should be paying his fair share? If so, you are providing a "safety net" that allows him to continue his addiction with no real consequences.

2. Refuse to cover up or make excuses for the person.

You might give rationales for why the addicted person can't attend family get-togethers or holiday parties ("She's feeling too sick to come"). You might whitewash rude or erratic behavior ("He's been under so much stress lately"). You might gloss over missed appointments or obligations ("I know she feels bad about it, but she's been incredibly busy").

YOU CAN'T CONTROL WHETHER SOMEONE SEEKS HELP FOR AN ADDICTION, BUT YOU CAN DECIDE WHAT KIND OF BEHAVIOR YOU WILL OR WILL NOT ACCEPT IN YOUR LIFE.

Helping to conceal the true behavior is not helping at all. That's because, once again, you are colluding to allow the person to escape consequences—and hard consequences are likely what is needed to shake your loved one out of denial.

3. Do not give or loan money.

Financial strain—especially if it's prolonged and desperate—is one of the consequences that can cause an addicted person to face reality. If you are providing money for any reason, you could be enabling the very behavior you want to end.

Setting financial limits might mean refusing to cosign loans, lend the person your own money, or pay bills to avoid repossession or eviction. It might mean looking for separate living arrangements or involve a promise that no more money is forthcoming. Whatever the step, it's an important one to take. When addictions become too expensive to maintain and funding sources are hard to come by, your loved one might finally get the help she needs.

4. Don't "rescue" the person when difficult consequences occur.

Rushing in to rescue the person may satisfy your desire to feel needed or helpful, but it doesn't really help the situation. It only cushions the blow or softens the landing for poor choices. In Al-Anon, they call it "putting pillows under them" so that the addict never feels the pain of mistakes.

5. Set boundaries and stick to them.

Family members often resort to saying things like, "If you don't quit drinking, I'll leave!" Or, "If you continue to use pornography, I'll ask you to live somewhere else." Or, "You've gambled away your car payment, and I'm not going to bail you out this time."

All of these are valid statements, but they are only idle, hollow threats unless you follow through with the "or else" part of the equation. You can't control whether someone seeks help for an addiction, but you can decide what kind of behavior you will or will not accept in your life.

BOUNDARIES

Personal boundaries are the physical, emotional, and mental limits we establish to protect ourselves from being manipulated, used, or violated by others. With boundaries, you are less likely to become entangled in the chaos of addiction, you will maintain order and dignity, and avoid emotional roller-coaster rides. Here are examples of boundaries:

"No drugs or alcohol are allowed around me or in the house."

Let your loved one know what substances are acceptable and unacceptable in the home. Then clearly explain the consequences if he or she violates those boundaries. Will you force her to find somewhere else to stay if she's been drinking? Will you notify the police if you find drugs in his room?

THE DISEASE OF ADDICTION THRIVES IN CHAOS AND LIES.

"I will not tolerate insults or put-downs."

You have the right to expect to be treated with respect others by others, including the addicted individual. In this way, you no longer sacrifice your self-worth. Re-establish the self-respect and integrity that you deserve, and that your family deserves, by defining what is acceptable language and behavior.

"I will not give you any more money, whether it is to pay a bill, buy you food, or put gas in your vehicle."

By setting the boundary to no longer financially support your loved one, you are focusing on your own well-being and mental health. You are also forcing him to take responsibility. Setting boundaries won't cure the addiction or control an addicted person, but they safeguard your mental health, physical well-being, and finances.

"I will not lie or cover for you anymore, regardless of the circumstances."

The disease of addiction thrives in chaos and lies. Set boundaries that will help remove you from the mayhem, and force your loved one to take ownership in his or her actions and behaviors.

"If you need an answer right now, the answer is no."

Addicts have a way of manipulating any situation. Oftentimes, this includes putting unnecessary stress and pressure on family members to make important decisions immediately. Most important decisions take time and prayer. If the addict in your life demands an answer, simply tell him or her no.

Compassion vs. Codependence

The danger is that some family members, wanting to avoid enabling and codependence, are fearful of showing *any* kindness, care, or compassion to the addict. This is a painful and frustrating way to live for all involved!

The truth is that to help your loved one, compassion is an essential ingredient. So how can you be caring toward someone with an addiction without falling into codependent, enabling behavior?

Understanding the definition of compassion is a great start. Here's what compassion is *not*:

- Covering for someone so they can continue their addiction without consequences.

- Eye-rolling, sighing, smirking, or other derogatory nonverbal gestures.

- Passive-aggressive behavior that allows you to "secretly" express your anger without confronting the addict about his or her behavior.

- Nagging or whining incessantly about the addict's behavior.

Now let's look at ways you can be compassionate in truth and grace—without enabling the problem.

Compassion is choosing not to lecture, guilt, or threaten.

You know the drill. A roll of the eyes, accompanied by a question or statement you've probably expressed a hundred times already:

- "I don't know why I put up with this."

- "Oh great, here we go again. Another day, another promise."

- "Why can't you get your life together? You're ruining your life—and mine."

- "When are you going to start acting like a man?"

You've said these things before—and they haven't helped. What makes you think they'll help now? The truth is that these kinds of statements never help and can add to the shame and self-loathing that is already fueling the addict's behavior.

Compassion is being aware and sympathetic toward the suffering of someone else.

You can be aware of—and even share in—the suffering of someone without trying to control or fix the person's pain. Perhaps you have grasped this concept as it applies to comforting someone who is grieving the death of a loved one. We are often told that one of the most compassionate things we can do for a mourning friend is just to be there: sit together, cry together, remember together. Grief is a hurt we simply can't fix or control for someone, no matter how much we love them. Sometimes all we can do is acknowledge their pain, and yet the therapeutic benefits of that are greater than we might imagine.

Think of your addicted loved one in a similar way. How can you acknowledge the pain they are in without trying to fix or control it for them? Perhaps you can simply listen, offer encouragement, or comfort with a touch or a hug. Look for ways to say "I know you are hurting" without taking on the impossible task of preventing or eliminating hurt for someone who is not ready to stop hurting himself.

Compassion is holding firm boundaries, for the addict's sake and for your sake too.

Some boundaries are easier to identify than others. For example, you may realize that saying yes to requests for money or requests to help an addict lie to avoid consequences is not helpful.

Other boundaries aren't as easy to identify. For example, one woman told her adult son not to call her after eleven at night. This came after years of middle-of-the-night phone calls during which the son, in tears, would verbally process all the pain and chaos in his life. Eventually the mother realized that the request her son repeatedly made of her was to be an unwitting participant in his self-destructive behavior. She also realized it was a request she needed to refuse. Answering the regular midnight calls might have seemed like the compassionate choice, but this crossed a line into unhealthy territory. She was helping to relieve his pain when he needed to experience it fully to see the need for change.

SAYING *NO* TO REQUESTS THAT ARE HARMFUL TO THE ADDICT— OR TO YOU—IS TRULY THE COMPASSIONATE APPROACH.

Compassion is letting go of any stigma you may be attaching to the problem.

Stigma is a negative belief held toward someone else. You might feel that your loved one's behavior has caused others to think poorly of you or your family. You might even have negative feelings yourself toward the addict in your life, verbalizing (or just thinking) shaming words or labels. If an addict—or the spouse, friends, or family of an addict—feels stigmatized, it adds to shame and hiding. Being honest with yourself and others about the addiction is essential to recovery and healing.

Ways to combat stigma include avoiding hurtful labels, seeking out supportive groups or people with whom you can safely share your story, and embracing the truth of God's Word that you are valuable and treasured no matter what others think.

Compassion is being willing to have uncomfortable conversations.

What's the best way to begin a conversation on a topic no one wants to address? You can broach the subject in a gentle, informal, and straightforward way. This is called a "soft intervention," and it is helpful when the addict in your life has not yet acknowledged the problem.

First, let me tell you what expectations and goals you should *not* have going into this conversation. It's not going to evoke a life change. It's not going to fix or cure the problem. It's not going to force someone into a recovery program. What this *can* do, however, is open dialogue, communicate your compassion and respect, begin to build trust, and start the process of dealing with reality. These are the elements of the conversation:

Affirmation: "I love you very much."

Always start and end with respect and support. You want to build a bridge of trust, and that bridge will only be built through love and affirmation, not blame, shame, or control.

Permission: "I have something important I'd like to talk to you about. Is that okay?"

In most situations, the person you are speaking to will say something like, "Um, sure, I guess so." Asking this question, however, invites participation. It shows respect. And it allows the persons to agree to at least have this conversation with you. In this manner, you are knocking on the door and asking to be invited in. You are not barging in with a head full of steam.

Observation: "I've noticed that when you come home, you start to drink alcohol and it continues through the night. This happens almost every night."

Make an observation, without accusation. Remember, the goal is to open conversation and build trust, so be intentional not to shame

YOU WANT TO BUILD A BRIDGE OF TRUST, AND THAT BRIDGE WILL ONLY BE BUILT THROUGH LOVE AND AFFIRMATION, NOT BLAME, SHAME, OR CONTROL.

> "DEAR BROTHERS AND SISTERS, IF ANOTHER BELIEVER IS OVERCOME BY SOME SIN, YOU WHO ARE GODLY SHOULD GENTLY AND HUMBLY HELP THAT PERSON BACK ONTO THE RIGHT PATH. AND BE CAREFUL NOT TO FALL INTO THE SAME TEMPTATION YOURSELF. SHARE EACH OTHER'S BURDENS, AND IN THIS WAY OBEY THE LAW OF CHRIST. ... WHENEVER WE HAVE THE OPPORTUNITY, WE SHOULD DO GOOD TO EVERYONE—ESPECIALLY TO THOSE IN THE FAMILY OF FAITH."
>
> Galatians 6:1-3, 10 NLT

or blame. And avoid "always" and "never" statements such as "You always get drunk and cause trouble" or "You never take responsibility." After all, the person you are talking to might remember a single exception to your word always or never and reject your entire statement as a result.

Invitation: "Can you tell me about that?"

Invite the person to share their thoughts and feelings on the matter. Remember, you don't have to agree with everything he says. The goal is not to get him to say what you want to hear (such as an apology or promise of change), but to invite sharing and build trust.

If your loved one doesn't want to talk about it, try to leave the door open a crack for a future conversation.

Follow-up: "I'd like to take this up again in the future."

If the conversation goes nowhere—with the person refusing to discuss the issue or getting defensive—resist the urge to become pushy or confrontational at this point. Instead, put the conversation on hold for now—but point out that you plan to follow up at a later time. This will help to defuse any tension that could be a major roadblock to discussion, while not letting go of the topic altogether. Don't wait too long to broach the topic again, perhaps bringing it up after a day or two.

By following these guidelines—compassion, permission, observation, invitation, follow-up—you've let your loved one know that you're concerned, that you love them enough to address the issue, and that you're willing to do so in love, without blaming or shaming.

CHAPTER 4

Supporting Your Loved One in Treatment and Beyond

It's possible (even likely) that your initial attempt to address the issue with your loved one has not produced the results you had hoped for. The person denied having a problem, refused to discuss it further, became defensive, got angry, deflected by saying you're overreacting, or "stonewalled" with the silent treatment. And your follow-up attempts have also gone nowhere. What then? It's time to consider a formal intervention.

In an intervention, family and close friends gather with the addicted person to discuss the issue. This is a meeting in which you face your loved one and explain your concerns about his health and well-being. You have probably seen these events portrayed in movies or TV shows, complete with shouting, swearing, and storming out of the room. Such depictions leave us thinking, *I'd never want to be a part of that! It looks awful!*

There's no sugarcoating the fact that an intervention is indeed full of emotion, usually uncomfortable for all involved, and often with tears flowing. It's a hard conversation! But it can also be hopeful, affirming, and loving.

How to Hold a Positive, Productive Intervention

In the past, experts advocated an aggressive, confrontational approach to interventions, advising friends and family members to begin by asking the addicted person to be quiet and listen. In this approach, the person was on the hot seat, with no say in the discussion and often given an ultimatum.

Many clinicians, including myself, now favor a more interactive approach, where the person can voice concerns without fear of reproach. Although the conversation must be direct, firm, and brutally honest, it can also be cooperative and honoring. Though confronted by hard truths and raw emotions, the person need not feel "ganged up on" or under siege.

By presenting the loved one with the realities and consequences of the addiction, an intervention might break through the person's denial and convince him to seek treatment. Hopefully you can direct the addict toward a doctor, rehab program, or support group that can help begin the recovery process.

An intervention typically involves the following steps.

1 Plan carefully.

Interventions require planning, thought, and specific attention to the addict's needs and circumstances. These encounters can be dramatic and emotionally charged, sometimes stirring up a sense of betrayal or resentment on the part of the addict. Therefore, you want to go into the meeting with a clear, step-by-step plan, leaving nothing to chance and no room for ad-libbing.

IT'S A HARD CONVERSATION! BUT IT CAN ALSO BE HOPEFUL, AFFIRMING, AND LOVING.

I strongly encourage you to enlist the help of an intervention specialist, who is usually a psychologist, counselor, or trained addiction expert. A professional interventionist can help you assemble the best team and construct the best plan. Such a specialist has been through the process many times and will

carefully walk you through each component of the intervention. Even if the specialist isn't present during the face-to-face meeting, he or she can equip you with the tools and resources to achieve a successful outcome.

2 Gather a team.

The people who participate in an intervention should be chosen with care. Only those who have a meaningful relationship with the addicted person are present. Acquaintances or anyone who might have an "agenda" should not be included. This isn't the time or place to mend fences or make a personal situation public.

There is no strict guideline about how many people should attend, though I recommend between six and twelve so as not to overwhelm the person being addressed. If the addict is a child, a parent typically leads the intervention team. If the addict is married or has a partner, the spouse typically leads.

Facing an addiction can be a lonely, frightening proposition. Seeing many friends and relatives who are willing to offer support may be just the encouragement the addict needs to begin the journey from brokenness to wholeness.

3   Decide on the best time and place.

Because of the sensitivity of the subject, the chances that your loved one may retaliate or react defensively are high. Be sure to approach him in a place that feels safe. Arrange the meeting at a time when emotions are calm and neutral instead of a situation where the environment is tense.

You want to talk to your loved one when he is sober—or as close to sober as possible. Talking to a person about addiction when he or she is high or impaired will be counterproductive. Drugs reduce a person's ability to think clearly, react calmly, and remember everything that's said.

It's tempting to hold an intervention in the family home. However, while you want your loved one to feel comfortable, home can be *too* comfortable. The person can retreat to a bedroom or bathroom when the conversation starts, and the talk could be over before it begins.

Holding an intervention in a neutral space—such as the office of a therapist or interventionist—is often the best option. People tend to be on their best behavior in these spaces, with less inclination to storm out when they're in new surroundings. Interventionists can help families to find a safe, private space. Families can also reach out to their churches or to community centers for assistance.

4 Hold rehearsals.

During an intervention, emotions can run high and people can easily veer off track or start rambling. Holding rehearsals makes it more likely to stay focused and avoid side issues. Practicing will help thoughts and words come out more clearly and concisely. Rehearsals can also help team members role-play and prepare for potential emotions or angry words from the individual with addiction.

> "IN THE END, PEOPLE APPRECIATE HONEST CRITICISM FAR MORE THAN FLATTERY."
>
> Proverbs 28:23 NLT

The number of rehearsals needed varies depending on the number of people involved and how those people feel about speaking up. It's wise to leave out people who can't commit to attending rehearsals. Practice is vital for the success of the intervention, so it's important for everyone to attend.

5 Stick to the script.

To communicate clearly and strongly, participants should consider creating a script, carefully preparing what they want to say. This is not the time to just "wing it" or speak what's on your heart at the moment.

Take the time the articulate precisely what you wish to communicate. You may revise this script multiple times as you talk with an interventionist, practice and polish what you want to say.

6 Share thoughts compassionately but directly.

Each member of the intervention team will speak during the intervention. This is meant to help the addict understand the concerns and feelings these team members have with regard to the addict's health and their own well-being.

When someone is addicted, that person may not see how the addiction is affecting others. They may be putting the addiction so much above everyone and everything around them that they're blinded to the effects, which is why personal stories and sharing during an intervention are so critical.

7 Strive to be hopeful.

Although the person should be told the unvarnished truth about the consequences of the addiction (damage to relationships, health, career, and so on), there is an opportunity to cast a vision for what life could be like and could become without the current problems. You can emphasize that addiction is an overwhelming obstacle and being free of it will create conditions for dreams to be achieved.

Also, keep the tone and style of conversation as positive as possible. How you talk to your loved one is almost as important as what you say. While conveying your thoughts, use warm body language, with eye contact and open posture.

8 State consequences if the person refuses help.

Often, the first time an addict encounters an intervention, the person will become defensive, angry, or silent, insisting there is no problem and refusing treatment of any kind. This response should be met with consequences that show how serious the intervention team is. Such consequences may include losing visitation rights with children, taking away the car, or asking the person to move out of the home.

ADMITTING TO THE PROBLEM IS THE FIRST STEP TOWARD RECOVERY.

These consequences need to be extremely specific and decided on in advance of the intervention. Everyone on the team should determine their own set of consequences.

9 | Present the treatment option.

Once every member of the intervention team has had a chance to speak, the addict should be presented with detailed suggestions for a treatment plan. Conduct research ahead of time, and come prepared to talk through specific options. The addict can accept the offer at the moment, or the team may be willing to give them a few days to weigh their options.

Treatment Options

If your loved one has acknowledged his struggle with addiction, you can breathe a prayer of gratitude. Admitting to the problem is the first step toward recovery. Yes, there's a long, challenging road ahead, but getting beyond denial clears a huge hurdle.

The next step is getting your loved one into a treatment program to help overcome physical and emotional dependency and restore overall well-being. You might start by consulting your physician, counselor, or pastor for referrals to local addiction-recovery specialists.

Your course of action will depend on the severity and duration of your loved one's addiction and should include one or more of the following options.

Detox

Those with severe forms of addiction may need to begin with a detox program prior to entering any kind of rehab. Detox enables the patient to safely withdraw from harmful substances until they are purged from their system. It is done on an inpatient basis in order to keep the patient from temptation and to closely monitor his response and overall health during the detoxification process.

Faith-based Treatment

You may prefer a Christian approach for your loved one's treatment, and there are now many faith-based organizations whose qualified Christian counselors and medical professionals offer a biblically based plan. Whether at a center, in therapy groups, or in one-on-one treatment, patients are surrounded by caring professionals who also have faith in God and his Word.

Inpatient Rehab

Usually necessary for those suffering from chronic addiction, these programs address the multiple facets of your loved one's battle for sobriety. Patients live in a substance-free facility and receive 24/7 monitoring, medical care, individual and group counseling, and life skills training. Narconon International strongly recommends inpatient programs longer than thirty days to give your loved one the best chance of both sobriety and life-skills development.[27]

Outpatient Rehab

With this option, the patient does not live in a treatment facility full-time. Rather, he attends scheduled treatment and life-skills training sessions during the week, enabling him to continue working or attend to family or other routine duties. However, because patients are not isolated from their usual surroundings, they are at greater exposure to the triggers that may cause them to backslide. Thus, outpatient rehab is more suitable for those with milder levels of addiction and who have made the commitment to overcoming their dependency. It is also a beneficial "next step" after inpatient treatment and can be helpful when combined with a future stay in a sober living home.

Support Groups

While completion of rehab or a sober living residence is a major accomplishment worth celebrating, the battle is far from over. Addiction is tenacious and tempting, so continued follow-up will be crucial to the long-term success of your loved one's recovery. A local support group, in which fellow strugglers share their stories and encourage one another, can motivate the recovering addict to choose sobriety in the days ahead. Twelve-step programs such as Alcoholics Anonymous and Narcotics Anonymous are available in nearly every community. Members are understanding and non-judgmental as they listen and encourage each other to stay committed to their recovery.

Sober Living Home

For those who need additional time, oversight, and accountability, a sober living home is a "residential bridge" in which the patient lives in a professionally supervised home with a handful of others in similar stages of recovery. Not as restrictive as inpatient rehab, these homes allow the patient a greater level of personal freedom while providing accountability, peer and professional support, and the ongoing reinforcement of healthy habits.

Addiction Counselors

Having a qualified professional counselor will lend considerable viability to the recovery process. An individual counselor can give your loved one personalized attention, encourage and guide her through her other treatment options, and custom-design a program for continuing aftercare.

Family Therapy

One family member's battle can pull an entire family into a state of confusion, resentment, embarrassment, fear, and fatigue. It is for weary family members that support groups such as Al-Anon and Nar-Anon were established: to help loved ones know they're not alone and to equip them with effective tools to ease the tension at home through improved coping and communication.

Life Skills Training

In the chaos of addiction, it's likely that your family member's practical life skills have suffered greatly. For this reason, treatment should include practical skills training—designed and slanted to the patient's age, gender, maturity, and level of recovery. Here are seven key life skills vital to successful re-entry into sober living.

1 Practicing Self-care

During and after recovery, re-establishing and prioritizing daily routines such as personal grooming, hygiene, keeping one's living space tidy, physical exercise, and Scripture reading and prayer will help regain a sense of order, inner peace, and self-esteem.

2 Handling Regular Responsibilities

Depending on the age, maturity, and living arrangement of your loved one, being entrusted with regular tasks can help him learn or re-learn responsibility and enjoy the feeling of effective life management. These can be relatively simple chores at first: taking out the trash, making the bed, tidying personal living space, or taking the dog for a walk.

(3) Developing a Routine

Tackling assigned tasks at approximately the same time each day alleviates procrastination and removes decision-making and stress from the process. Faithful attendance at support groups or therapy sessions will be boosted if the sessions are held at the same day and time each week. Living by a routine helps good habits become more automatic and less likely to slip.

(4) Time Management

This skill can be tough for those in recovery, mainly because their lives have been focused on nurturing the addiction rather than on family, work, school, or personal well-being. A small daily calendar with time slots for each hour is a helpful tool in which counseling appointments, support group meetings, chores, physical workouts, church services, work or school, and other key activities can be scheduled a week or two in advance.

(5) Handling Finances

Financial management training for recovering young people helps them learn about living within their means, opening and servicing checking and savings accounts, controlling debt, and managing credit cards. For adults, relearning financial responsibility means a major change in cash flow: from feeding their addiction to paying for housing, utilities, insurance, groceries, and other living costs.

6 Stress Management

Recognizing stress as a detrimental trigger is a critical skill for those in recovery, because stress can agitate addictive desires and lead to possible relapse. Stress management training teaches patients to recognize and resist their triggers through deep breathing, strenuous walking, attending a support group, prayer, or reaching out to a trusted friend.

7 Building Healthy, Stable Relationships

Elysia Richardson, writing for Pathway to Hope, notes, "People who are new in recovery may find that they have to start over with new friends. ... It's necessary to associate with people who share the same goals and support a new life of sobriety."[28] Your recovering loved one will need to say no to harmful relationships while establishing healthy new ones. They need to surround themselves with positive people who will only encourage and affirm them in their new disciplines. Support groups and church groups can be of significant help in forming new, recovery-enabling friendships.

Before you enroll a family member in treatment, especially in a residential-type program, be sure to inquire if they provide life skills training and what, specifically, is included in the curriculum.

What Are the Chances of Relapse?

First, the bad news: Relapse is a tough reality of the recovery process. It happens in a high percentage of cases, so don't be shocked if your family member relapses and don't consider him—or yourself—a failure.

> "BE JOYFUL IN HOPE,
> PATIENT IN AFFLICTION,
> FAITHFUL IN PRAYER."
>
> Romans 12:12

Now the good news: If you and your loved one stay diligent with the recovery and aftercare program, chances of eventual success are good.

Relapse is typically caused by exposure to people, places, stresses, and emotions that remind the patient of his or her addictive practices. These triggers cause intense physical or psychological cravings, and the recovering addict thinks he needs alcohol, drugs, or re-indulgence in his harmful behavior in order to calm the emotional upheaval.

According to the National Institute on Drug Abuse, between 40 and 60 percent of those in recovery from drug addiction will relapse.[29] It is most common during a person's first year of recovery, which underscores the importance of continued aftercare following the initial treatment program. But relapse can occur anytime, even after years of sobriety, and it's important to keep in mind that if relapse happens, it doesn't mean the battle is lost. Determine to learn from any relapse; it can teach valuable lessons about what can be done next time to strengthen the chances of long-term success.

Addiction-recovery specialists generally agree on these five "best practices" to help someone avoid relapse.

1 Avoid triggering situations.

A helpful exercise is for your loved one to write out a list of people, places, emotions, and situations that have triggered addictive indulgence in the past. Being aware of the triggers will help your loved one recognize and stand strong against potentially tempting situations as they arise in the future.

2 Be diligent with follow-up therapy.

Regular participation in a support group should be high priority. The same goes for appointments with a personal therapist. Both will offer ongoing encouragement, support, and gentle correction during recovery and challenging times.

3 Get rid of toxic friends.

It's critical that your loved one "unfriend" and steer clear of those who accompanied and were associated with the addictive behavior. Social pressure is a tough influence to overcome, and it's crucial that someone in recovery replace toxic friends with a positive support network.

4 Develop a positive support network.

Your loved one needs healthy people around to uplift, encourage, pray for, and affirm him during the journey. Non-toxic friends can help him avoid and overcome triggers, accompany him to sober entertainment or recreational activities, and serve as a listening ear. Family, friends, support groups, small groups at church, Bible studies, classes, and other positive environments offer good possibilities for finding and developing nourishing relationships.

5 Stay on prescribed medications.

Addiction and addiction recovery are often accompanied (and exacerbated by) other illnesses such as anxiety or depression. This is called "dual diagnosis." If the treating physician has prescribed medication for an accompanying illness, your loved one should be diligent in taking the medications as prescribed. This is crucial to his mental and emotional health and in his resolve to prevent relapse.

Support Groups

Perhaps the best way for you and your family to support your loved during treatment and recovery is to take part in a local support group for friends and families of addicts. Earlier I mentioned AA and Al-Anon, national organizations that offer hundreds of local support groups as well as online information to help strengthen, equip, and guide those who have a loved one in treatment or recovery. You may also find helpful faith-based support groups through your church. (See *Recommended Resources* at the back of this book.)

STRENGTH, LOVE, AND AFFIRMATION ARE THE KEYS.

Support groups and supportive friends empower you to come alongside your loved one from a position of strength, love, and calm. The last thing a recovering addict needs is a family member who tries to nag, demean, or embarrass him into better behavior. Such negative motivation will only create resistance and could even spur a relapse. Your recovering loved one needs positive motivation of affirmation and praise for his willingness to change. He needs your help and example with healthy meals and snacks. If he hesitates on a life-skills task such as making his bed, filling out his calendar, or paying bills, you might say, "Here, I'll do it with you" and tackle the task together. (Of course, do not do it for him.) Your goal is to equip and empower him for positive behavior and not to enable poor behavior. Strength, love, and affirmation are the keys.

> "FOR WE DO NOT HAVE A HIGH PRIEST WHO IS UNABLE TO EMPATHIZE WITH OUR WEAKNESSES, BUT WE HAVE ONE [CHRIST JESUS] WHO HAS BEEN TEMPTED IN EVERY WAY, JUST AS WE ARE—YET HE DID NOT SIN. LET US THEN APPROACH GOD'S THRONE OF GRACE WITH CONFIDENCE, SO THAT WE MAY RECEIVE MERCY AND FIND GRACE TO HELP US IN OUR TIME OF NEED."
>
> Hebrews 4:15-16

Yes, it's a long, tough journey. There will be ups and there will be downs. But stay strong. With God's help, a positive support network, a ton of love and patience, and the tools I'm sharing with you, you can do this. You can help your loved one find wholeness and enjoy a healthy, fruitful life.

A Closing Word

"Why hasn't God answered my prayers?"

That question came from Lauren, a thirty-five-year-old client who had struggled with opioid addiction for a decade. Her words seemed to communicate hope and despair, optimism and frustration. As a mental health professional guided by my Christian faith, spirituality has always been a component of my whole-person approach. Addiction and recovery, in my experience, touch deeply into spiritual matters.

Addiction can take on a life of its own and create a sense of powerlessness in those addicted—and those who love them. Is it any wonder, then, that people seek out something or someone greater than themselves to help them overcome the power of addiction? Nowhere is this principle better demonstrated than in the twelve steps from Alcoholics Anonymous, so many of which speak directly to the role of spirituality, faith, and belief in God as a cornerstone to recovery.

As I said before, addiction is jealous. It does not want anything to get in the way of its power over a person. As such, addiction can create an atmosphere of shame, worthlessness, and guilt in those who are addicted. Addiction is not beyond using a person's faith as a weapon against them, telling the person they are irredeemable, unworthy of forgiveness, and doomed to condemnation. Addiction seeks to speak with a distortion of God's voice, denying faith's promise of acceptance, forgiveness, and redemption.

ADDICTION SEEKS TO SPEAK WITH A DISTORTION OF GOD'S VOICE, DENYING FAITH'S PROMISE OF ACCEPTANCE, FORGIVENESS, AND REDEMPTION.

I asked Lauren to consider that God had, indeed, answered her prayers, as she was at The Center, in treatment, with the possibility of learning more about herself, her addiction, and the power of God to heal. I perceived she wanted a lightning strike, a bolt of faith that would come down from heaven and remove her addiction. I asked her if that was true.

Lauren sat quietly for a minute, pondering my question. She finally replied, "I suppose that is true. I just want God step in, heal my struggles, and make everything okay. I'm just so tired that I want God to take away my addiction once and for all."

I explained that through the years I have occasionally seen such immediate and spectacular things happen. And I know it's in God's power to do miracles in our world today, even curing a disease like addiction. But almost always, I have seen healing happen over time, as people slowly and painstakingly walked step by step through the recovery process. I commented that even Christ walked a path to the cross, which involved suffering and, ultimately, victory.

People struggling with addiction and the family members desperate to help them need to continually be reminded that God can provide the strength, courage, and hope to press on through the demanding journey toward wellness. As Scripture assures us …

- "Be strong and courageous. Do not be afraid or terrified because of them, for the LORD your God goes with you; he will never leave you nor forsake you" (Deuteronomy 31:6).

- "But he said to me, 'My grace is sufficient for you, for my power is made perfect in weakness.'

Therefore I will boast all the more gladly about my weaknesses, so that Christ's power may rest on me. That is why, for Christ's sake, I delight in weaknesses, in insults, in hardships, in persecutions, in difficulties. For when I am weak, then I am strong" (2 Corinthians 12:9–10).

- "I can do all this through him who gives me strength" (Philippians 4:13).

Faith, which is the confidence in what we hope for and assurance about what we do not see, can act as the forward vision that sees beyond the devastation of the addiction (see Hebrews 11:1). Without that forward vision, the landscape is littered with the wreckage of the addiction, which seems impossible to overcome.

Trust in God assures you that your loved one can indeed overcome addiction and go on to live a full, healthy, contented life. And your relationship with this family member—though perhaps strained or even broken at the moment—can once again achieve stability and harmony.

I say all of this with utmost confidence and conviction, because God is much bigger than any addiction or associated problems, no matter how daunting. God will supply all of the strength, peace, and wisdom you need to carry you through this very difficult time. God is on your side!

Recommended Resources

Books

Beyond Addiction: How Science and Kindness Help People Change by Jeffrey Foote, et. al. (Scribner, 2014)

Boundaries: When to Say Yes, How to Say No to Take Control of Your Life by John Townsend and Henry Cloud (Zondervan, 2017)

The Complete Family Guide to Addiction: Everything You Need to Know Now to Help Your Loved One and Yourself by Thomas F. Harrison and Hilary S. Connery (Guilford Press, 2019)

Don't Call It Love: Breaking the Cycle of Relationship Dependency by Gregory L. Jantz and Tim Clinton (Revell, 2015)

Healing the Scars of Addiction: Reclaiming Your Life and Moving Into a Healthy Future by Gregory L. Jantz (Revell, 2018)

Unspoken Legacy: Addressing the Impact of Trauma and Addiction in the Family by Claudia Black (Central Recovery Press, 2018)

When Your Partner Has An Addiction by Christopher Lawson (BenBella Books, 2016)

Information, Resources, and Helplines

Substance Abuse and Mental Health Service
Administration (SAMHSA) www.samhsa.gov
(800) 622-HELP (4357)

American Addiction Centers
www.americanaddictioncenters.org

National Institute on Alcohol Abuse and Alcoholism
www.niaaa.nih.gov

The National Institute on Drug Abuse www.nida.org

Partnership to End Addiction www.drugfree.org

Self-Help Groups for Addiction

Alcoholics Anonymous
www.alcoholics-anonymous.org

Chemically Dependent Anonymous
www.cdaweb.org

Marijuana Anonymous
www.marijuana-anonymous.org

Methadone Anonymous
www.methadone-anonymous.org

Narcotics Anonymous
www.na.org

Self-Compassion
www.mindfulselfcompassion.org

Gamblers Anonymous
www.gamblersanonymous.org

Overeaters Anonymous
www.oa.org

Groups to Support Loved Ones

Al-Anon. A worldwide fellowship that offers a program of recovery for the families and friends of alcoholics. www.al-anon.org

Co-Anon. For family members and friends of someone who is addicted to cocaine or other mind-altering substances. www.co-anon.org

Families Anonymous. A twelve-step fellowship for the family and friends of individuals with drug, alcohol, or related behavioral issues. www.familiesanonymous.org

Nar-Anon. For relatives and friends affected by someone else's addiction. www.nar-anon.org

Christian Recovery Organizations

American Association of Christian Counselors. Equips clinical, pastoral, and lay caregivers with biblical truth and psychosocial insights that minister to hurting persons and helps them move to personal wholeness. Referral service for local counselors, coaches, and clinics. (800) 526-8673 www.aacc.net

Celebrate Recovery. A Christ-centered, twelve-step recovery program for anyone struggling with hurt, pain, or addiction of any kind. www.celebraterecovery.com

Faith in Recovery. This non-denominational Christ-centered, faith-based program assists those who are suffering from drug and alcohol addiction or mental health disorders. www.faithinrecovery.com

National Association for Christian Recovery. Provides faith-based tools, articles, and classes for individuals (and family members) struggling with addiction. www.nacr.org

Notes

1   Created for the Houston chapter of Al-Anon by Sara Wartes (2010).

2   "What Is Addiction?" American Psychiatric Association. *www.psychiatry.org/patients-families/addiction/what-is-addiction.*

3   "Definition of Addiction," American Society of Addiction Medicine (ASAM). *www.asam.org/quality-practice/definition-of-addiction.*

4   Seyyed Salman Alavi, et al., "Behavioral Addiction versus Substance Addiction: Correspondence of Psychiatric and Psychological Views," International Journal of Preventive Medicine 3 (April 2012): 290–294.

5   "CAGE Questionnaire," Wikipedia, last modified September 26, 2017. *https://en.wikipedia.org/wiki/CAGE_questionnaire.*

6   "Screening Tests," National Institute on Alcohol Abuse and Alcoholism. *https://pubs.niaaa.nih.gov/publications/arh28-2/78-79.htm.*

7   Presentation by Nora D. Volkow, M.D. to the Senate Caucus on International Narcotic Control, "America's Addiction to Opioids: Heroin and Prescription Drug Abuse," May 4, 2014. *https://archives.drugabuse.gov/testimonies/2014/americas-addiction-to-opioids-heroin-prescription-drug-abuse.*

8   "Prescription Drugs and Cold Medicines," National Institute on Drug Abuse. *www.drugabuse.gov/drugs-abuse/prescription-drugs-cold-medicines* (accessed December 5, 2017).

9   Lia Steakley, "Report Shows over 60 Percent of Americans
    Don't Follow Doctors' Orders in Taking Prescription Meds,"
    Stanford Medicine, April 25, 2012, *http://scopeblog.stanford
    .edu/2012/04/25/report-shows-over-60-percent-of-americans
    -dont-follow-doctors-orders-in-taking-prescription-meds.*

10 "Current Cigarette Smoking among Adults in the United
    States," Centers for Disease Control and Prevention.
    December 1, 2016. *www.cdc.gov/tobacco/data_statistics/
    fact_sheets/adult_data/cig_smoking.*

11 "Eating Disorder Statistics," National Association of
    Anorexia Nervosa and Associated Disorders. *www.anad.org*
    (accessed January 8, 2017).

12 Vera Nezgovorova et. al., "Problematic Internet Use and Its
    Impact on Anxiety, Depression, and Addiction," Anxiety and
    Depression Association of America. *https://adaa.org/learn
    -from-us/from-the-experts/blog-posts/professional/
    problematic-internet-use-and-its-impact.*

13 Meredith Somers, "More than Half of Christian Men Admit
    to Watching Pornography," Washington Times, August 24,
    2014.

14 "Making the Connection: Trauma and Substance Abuse,"
    The National Child Traumatic Stress Network (NCTSN),
    June 2008.

15 Michael G. Pipich, "The Bipolar-Addiction Connection,"
    Psychology Today (September 10, 2018).

16 "Dopamine and Addiction: Separating Myths and Facts,"
    Healthline.com. *www.healthline.com/health/dopamine
    -addiction#motivation.*

17 "Genetics and Epigenetics of Addiction," National Institute on Drug Abuse. Last updated February 2016. *www.drugabuse.gov/publications/drugfacts/genetics-epigenetics-addiction*.

18 "Statistics on Addiction in America," Addiction Center. *www.addictioncenter.com/addiction/addiction-statistics*.

19 "Definition of Addiction," American Society of Addiction Medicine. *www.asam.org/quality-practice/definition-of-addiction*.

20 Dan Mager, "Addiction as a Family Affliction," *Psychology Today* (May 2, 2016).

21 Ron Breazeale, "Catastrophic Thinking," *Psychology Today* (March 25, 2011).

22 Brené Brown, "Shame v. Guilt," January 14, 2013. *https://brenebrown.com/blog/2013/01/14/shame-v-guilt*.

23 "Family Disease," National Council on Alcoholism and Drug Dependence (February 24, 2016).

24 John Gramlich, "Nearly half of Americans have a family member or close friend who's been addicted to drugs," Pew Research Center. October 26, 2017. *www.pewresearch.org/fact-tank/2017/10/26/nearly-half-of-americans-have-a-family-member-or-close-friend-whos-been-addicted-to-drugs*.

25 "Caregiver stress: Tips for taking care of yourself," Mayo Clinic. *www.mayoclinic.org/healthy-lifestyle/stress-management/in-depth/caregiver-stress/art-20044784*.

26 Jeffrey Foote, Carrie Wilkens, Nicole Kosanke, and Stephanie Higgs, Beyond Addiction: How Science and Kindness Help People Change (Scribner, 2014).

27 "Do's and Don'ts for Dealing with an Addict in Your Life," Narconon. *www.narconon.org/blog/drug-addiction/dos-donts -dealing-addict-life*.

28 Elysia Richardson, "10 Life Skills Essential to Recovery," Pathway to Hope. November 8, 2019. *https:// pathwaytohope.net/blog/life-after-addiction*.

29 "Drugs, Brains, and Behavior: The Science of Addiction: Treatment and Recovery," National Institute on Drug Abuse. July 2020. *www.drugabuse.gov/publications/drugs -brains-behavior-science-addiction/treatment-recovery*.

MORE RESOURCES FROM DR. GREGORY L. JANTZ

Unmasking Emotional Abuse: Start the Healing

Six Steps to Reduce Stress

Ten Tips for Parenting the Smartphone Generation

Five Keys to Dealing with Depression

Five Keys to Health and Healing: Hope for Body, Mind, and Spirit

Seven Answers for Anxiety

Five Keys to Raising Boys

40 Answers for Teens' Top Questions

When a Loved One Is Addicted: How to Offer Hope and Help

Social Media and Depression: How to be Health and Happy in the Digital Age

www.hendricksonrose.com